GRIM

Kate Newmann

GRIM

ARLEN
HOUSE

Grim

is published in 2015 by
ARLEN HOUSE
42 Grange Abbey Road
Baldoyle
Dublin 13
Ireland
Phone/Fax: 353 86 8207617
Email: arlenhouse@gmail.com
arlenhouse.blogspot.com

Distributed internationally by
SYRACUSE UNIVERSITY PRESS
621 Skytop Road, Suite 110
Syracuse, NY 13244–5290
Phone: 315–443–5534/Fax: 315–443–5545
Email: supress@syr.edu

978–1–85132–120–9, paperback

Typesetting by Arlen House
Printed lithographically in Dublin
Cover image: 'The Crucifixion' by J.B. Vallely
is reproduced by permission of the artist

CONTENTS

ACKNOWLEDGEMENTS

I am grateful to Paula Meehan, John Kerrigan, Angus Adamson, Theodore Deppe, Stephen Fry, Adrian O'Byrne, Annie Deppe, Audrey Weir, Cathal Ó Searcaigh, Gary Price, Shay O'Byrne, Brian Patten, Maria McManus, Anna Prokovnik, Stephen Coles, Susann Huschke, Joscha Lemke, Damian Gorman and Colum Sands for responding to the poems as they were being written, to *The Stinging Fly* for having published 'Göring and Göring' and to J.B. Vallely for his permission to reproduce his painting, 'The Crucifixion'.

I wish to thank the Arts Council/An Chomhairle Ealaíon for awarding me a bursary.

WORK SETS YOU FREE

The time it takes to read these
sixteen poems is approximately the
time it takes to die in a gas chamber

1

PHOTOGRAPHER

Portraits line the corridor
in simple frames,
front-on as for a passport
and in profile.

Some of the women
are almost smiling,
already rendered naked
in that flash of trust.

The photographer must have kept his eyes open.
He must have instructed them
to keep their eyes open
as his deft deliberate finger

triggered the shutter's eye
to close blankly, briefly,
against the brutality.
Caught here by him

in the black and white
of this time and this place,
what happened
will always be about to happen

to the children,
to the men,
to the women
who hold our gaze.

2

MUSIC

March: A strongly rhythmical
piece in duple or quadruple time.
Apt for processional purposes.

Auschwitz was unique:
a work camp, a prison camp
and an extermination camp.

Twice a day the strong were marched
rhythmically under *Arbeit Macht Frei,*
Work Sets You Free: the old joke
soldered above the gate in wrought iron
(when the only way out, the guide says,
was as smoke up the chimney).

It is still there, the flat area
where the orchestra played marches.
Easier to count them out.
To count them in.

A fanfare each morning, each evening.
The steps of prisoners falling in behind the bars,
the mathematics of music adding
to the mathematics of death, mounting
past the unbearable pitch to where
we can no longer hear
the frequency of heartbeats –
dominants, subdominants, leading note
and answering phrase,
slurred with living hate until
the scale of it deadens us.

3

DON'T ASK

Why they didn't rise up.
Why they didn't escape.

The mock trials, the secret
executions were blacked out
from view by boarded windows.
The hooks where prisoners
hung by their hands,
arms twisted behind their backs
like fractured wings.
The 'wall of death' where
it took just one soldier
to hold up two defeated victims
as they were shot
through the back of the neck.

Only the 'execution' of escapees.
That was very public.
And until the prisoner was found,
until the prisoner was recaptured,

relatives and friends
were rounded up and brought in
to stand in the open in the prison
at the mercy …

4

AFTER QUARANTINE

It hurts a tree
when you carve into its bark.
It damages the cambium layer,
though the wood will grow
smoothing over the edges
as the letters warp and change
with the tree's slow thrust
away from the earth.

One survivor, a number gouged
the whole length of her thigh.
Her forearm wasn't long enough.
The six digits wouldn't fit.
Because she was tattooed as a baby.

5

BLOCK 10

Here in Block 10 there were medical experiments.
If women survived, they were savagely injured.
It was part of the plan to sterilise
'undesirables' and to create a superior race
who would breed twins.
It was the psychology of agriculture
and animal husbandry taken to its chill conclusion.

I had thought our guide unfeeling.
I had thought her cold.
But she was right.
There is no fit metre, no worthy metaphor.
Just say it into the birdless air:

Many died here.
Most children were exterminated.
Twins and siblings
were kept alive
for experiments.
Pregnant women
and small babies.
Otherwise they were
gassed on entry.

6

CELLS

There is a universal language,
an Esperanto of cruelty
– the hunger cell, the dark cell –
which closes in on the senses.

In every country there must be
a prison wall where someone
has scratched their existence
into stone or into plaster.

A hare in the wild
ranges freely over eleven square kilomctres.
In the tiny cell – it is smaller than
a telephone box – four people
had to stand the entire suffocating night,
their thoughts a failed graffiti
scored into the shallow-breathing dark.

7

PLAYING MENGELE

When Auschwitz fell
one surviving child
was fostered.

She would line up her friends
then choose one at random.
That was the game.
Playing Mengele – who
would be chosen for experiments
this day.

An Argentinian man on the tour
explains he cannot understand English well.
He tells the guide he lived near Mengele
in Argentina. *I have heard*, she says,
about the Nazi village with its beautiful flowers.

Yes, beautiful, he agrees. I loathe him
on the bus back to Krakow
as he snores with his mouth open.

If there was more to the game, *Playing Mengele*,
the adults never saw.

8

WALLS HAVE A MEMORY

This room, the guide says,
has been left as it was —
the floor, the walls.
It feels like any bleak provincial barracks.
If we didn't know.
But there are radiators! someone says.

Yes, they were here already.
It was a Polish military base.
The heating system was here.
But it wasn't used.

9

ZYKLON B

Death is not such an easy accomplice.
There were experiments with Zyklon B.
The poison came in tins, spilled out
like pellets you might put down for rats.

Ten to twelve tins (am I remembering this
correctly?) could kill one thousand one hundred people.

But it took the collusion of body heat
– the self's involuntary urge to live –
to release the cyanide into the atmosphere.

In this building, the soldiers poured
Zyklon B pellets onto the floor
then ran.
On re-entering, they found
some prisoners still alive.

They poured out twice the amount.
This time it worked.
The perfect balance.
Body heat co-operating with death.

10

LOST

I can't remember the order.
I don't know when
we stare, frozen,
at the bone-white architect's model
preparing us for Birkenau
and what no longer exists
– somewhere between an architect's model
and a doll's house, with
made-to-scale people –
but it hardly matters
as we hear
how these tiny model people
were told they were going to shower.
Told to leave all belongings
except little personal items.
Told to get undressed and
– odd how a beam of anger can light on one small moment –
told to leave all their clothes
on a *numbered* coat hanger
and told to remember their number.
Told to take a towel and a toothbrush
if they had one.
And not to forget their number.

11

COLLUSION

I cannot understand
how the eyes and the fingers
of the 'special commandoes'
were so complicit.

Responsible for bringing out the bodies.
Still warm.
Cutting off the hair.
Removing rings, earrings, chains
and gold teeth.

After three months
these prisoners,
as eye-witnesses,
were exterminated.
And replaced.
One survived
– a Greek
living in Venice –
to write his memories.

It's not his conscience I want to blame.
It's his complying hands.

They even had to search
in intimate places
where people sometimes
hid their jewellery.

12

ROOMS OF AFTERMATH

Of course – this is just a fraction
of what the Russian troops found
when relieving the camp.

It's true that we cannot comprehend,
cannot, literally, take in
anything but the singular dying.

So these rooms of aftermath
diminish to an abstract poignancy:

a mound of pots and pans and shaving brushes
shining like found flint with the patina
of their owners' hands;

a pile of spectacle frames,
each memorising the curve of the ear,
unfocus us.

The stack of artificial limbs
like theatre props.

They make macabre sculptures
as though to prove that there is no such thing
as miracle. Nothing,
when it comes to it,
to save us.

So many shoes.

13

NOTHING WENT TO WASTE

I imagined a fur farm.
Arctic foxes kept in cages.
The breathing, bloody, feeling bodies
just a means of growing
the harvest of pelts.

Human hair was sent to textile factories.
It was carded, spun, woven
into cloth, into ropes.
It was used to stuff mattresses
on which other people
made love and slept and prayed and dreamed.
It was used as padding inside uniforms
to keep soldiers warm.

There is a room full of it.
Piled, wiry, like sheep's wool.
A woman who saw it in 1947
was dismayed when she returned last year.
It was all colours back then.

Still hostage to time.
An entire room of hair
turning grey.

14

SUITCASES

You can't smell the old leather
of the stacked suitcases,
the naphthalene echoes,
the mothy linings
emptied of everything
but their heavy irony.

A few names are visible – all that's left
as record (words are evidence and
documents were destroyed on arrival).

There – my gut lurches – my name.
Neumann. Twice.
Friedrich Neumann and Rene Neumann.
I know from my mother that my father was circumcised.
I know from my father that my grandfather was circumcised.
But I know my chromosomes
could just as easily be descended
from a man who shot dead an escapee
for the reward of three days' leave.

And I won't allow myself that slipstream of emotion,
that claim to feeling,
simply because this horror
happened to people
who might be part of me.

It's not enough.

None of us are feeling enough.

15

LIKE AN ABATTOIR

There is an engine roaring in my head
the way it roared
outside the gas chamber
to drown out the screams.

It took twenty minutes approximately.
Zyklon B and body heat and the realisation dawning.

I don't want to write
how it was like being herded into a low byre,
how it collapsed the lungs,
how, broken down past memory and prayer,
all of you becomes one ferocious need
to get out of there.

16

ANIMAL VEGETABLE MINERAL

Families of Polish political prisoners
could pay vast sums
to buy back the ashes.
It was very controversial.
There was great doubt
whose ashes they received.

Ashes were dumped in lakes
which closed over them with a stupor of sky.

Some were spread as fertiliser
to grow food in the unasking fields;
the soil grainy with a wraith of bonemeal.
Everything we've dreamed, compostable.

Somewhere there are oranges
and moths the mottle of tree bark.
Somewhere the words 'turmeric' and 'cumin'
are grinding to an aromatic halt.

Above the spice mill
in the terrified eaves
Anne Frank's family
lose the habit of speech.

The wallpaper is stained copper beech.
Anne pins up Ginger Rogers, Leonardo da Vinci,
the chimpanzees' tea party in London Zoo.

The walls have taught her
how to stay *bladstil* – still as a leaf.
For days she eats boiled lettuce
which wilts to an unsayable sludge.

She has already filled the margins,
written across the canals of memory
in both directions. The walls abridge it all.

The floor is a ration book.
She exchanges her valerianed footfall
for a rectangle of stifle.

Pale, she bleaches the fine hair
on her upper lip
and is glad, when through the membrane of despair
her monthly cycle returns:
the body's ludicrous trust
in its own future.

Her nerves have learnt
a faltering night cadenza,
her hands moving over
the soft refrain of her breasts.

Across the chairs where she sleeps
there is no room for the heart's octaves
to stretch out
only the small dance of lungs, pulse, gut
and the mortifying timpani of peeing in a pot.

Sometimes earth collaborates
and smuggles in a glut of ripening.
So many peas – their shelled monosyllables
pocking into the bowl,

Anne thumbing out the flesh
from each pod, leaving a daze
of veined translucence;
the smell, indoors, of country rain.

And watching her father
bottle what is to come
in the colour red;
boiling the strawberries
a second time
for fear of them going to waste.

Somewhere, a woman cycles
across Amsterdam
in heavy fog,
a bag of oranges
secreted.

Somewhere a man – not a Jew –
who sold her the oranges

and never asked.
Somewhere shadows rounded up,
bullied back into human form.

Somewhere the man is in a cattle truck.
The man who sold the oranges
locked in a cattle truck for days.
Somewhere he is coming to answer a door slowly,
both his legs lost through frostbite.

Above in the attic
a hand closes over the pitted planet
of an orange's outrageous wholeness,
too zest, too pith,
too flesh to bear.

USELESS EATERS
Independent, 5 and 27 January 2013

Anyone with 'disability'
physical or mental;
anyone with an illness
deemed hereditary.

These people were considered
'unworthy of life'. 'Useless Eaters'.
Those were the words
inked beside their names.

Midwives had to report
any newborn babies
with imperfections.
Children and adults

were placed in the hands
of the Berlin Charitable Foundation
for Cure and Institutional Care
who discreetly, with official composure,

instructed that they be
starved to death in rooms
or injected with lethal poison.
The families of these people

received a letter
of condolence, an urn
of ashes and
a faked death certificate.

In 1940 the regime developed vans
with sealed compartments
where carbon monoxide
could suffocate people in less than half an hour.

It must have taken
a long time for patients
to shuffle down stuffy corridors
their faces turned in trust

to nurses in white coats
who told them
You're going on an outing. You're going on an outing,
and helped them into the van.

It needs a new and slurring language
banging its head against a wall
in frustration at the slobbery words
which won't say themselves.

But over 275,000
'undesirables' were killed;
their lives, and then their deaths
kept soundproofed from society.

Walter Rauff,
who designed the 'mobile gas chamber'
lived, until 1985, in Santiago, Chile,
no more regretful than any retired industrialist,

drinking beer and dining on beef steaks,
apricots, cherries, pisco sour.

THE HUNGRY EYE
Leni Riefenstahl, cinematographer for the Third Reich

Once, her eyes let her down.
In a village in Poland she saw German soldiers
forcing thirty civilians to dig their own deep grave.

She did not stay to focus
on the forearms straining like oarsmen,
close-up montage,
veins distended in a forehead,
shovel handle like a crucifix,
their fresh loamy horizon at terrible eye level.

The cameo turned bloody before she turned away
and was trapped, grimacing, just once
on the wrong side of the cold sensibility of lens.

She could not choreograph the clouds
but she could filter the sky
and bring a camera so low
that Hitler's torso loomed upright – rostra, podia –
the capital I of *ICH* merging
with the dream of madness
as though it was all inevitable.

And looking down on everything
she showed the plane which carried him,
its shadow, as god signs;
the heads of those below
like iron filings moving beneath
a magnet's pull. She found a distance
from where conscience, in a crowd, was invisible.

At night, she knew Goebbels
sat with a censor's green pencil
raised over every film script,

every piece of planned footage.
His letter to an early lover
might have been sent to her:
'I would make you love me
for a moment. Then I would kill you'.

She had trained her camera
into the Führer's eyes; seen back past the mustard gas
that taught him in the trenches,
to the serenity that used to settle
as he made sketches of obedient dogs,
all benign and cross-hatched mediocrity.

Leni and Adolf had a covenant –
they could decide
what bodies were going to mean.

She used her own limbs as reconnaissance,
so when it came to filming the Olympics
she was ravenous for this language with no words
and knew every nuance
of pectoral muscles; the strange bony imperfection of knees;
beads of sweat; clenched jaws; chiaroscuro of an Adam's
    apple,
in cinematic slow-down, in restaged second attempts,
swivelling, hand-held – earlobes; epidermis; body hair;
creased brow; a gasp; mouths open in concentration;
    the trajectory
of an arched spine; the frightening tempo; the chaos
of physical strain; pulsing temples; tight muscles; sheer
exhaustion. Runners pitted against each other
and their own shadows.

Not the gangly limbs of the champion high jumper,
Gretel Bergmann, excluded
                    because
                        because.

Rolls of negative hanging
like rope ladders climbing away from the ugly.
Chosen truths packed in canisters.
All the pathos curling like wood shavings
on the cutting room floor.

No filament of contrition.
She lived until she was one hundred and one.
When you die, the eyes are the first to putrefy –
grey, deliquescent, flecked as damaged celluloid
with everything you didn't care to see.

'WHY SUFFER?'
Otto and Elise Hampel, d. 1943
Guardian, 8 January 2011 and *Irish Times*, 21 April 2012

It was hard to breathe the cryptic air
in the tight room, with Elise mothering
her dead brother, killed in the German
army, her always nursing his too-soon,
too-soon, like an injured hedgehog.

It was hard to breathe in the tight city,
the flat denying air, with ordinary
people everywhere stupid with fear. It
was easier than doing nothing. So Otto
rebelled against the Führer,

became a comrade with words. He
devoted himself like a Brechtian
character, to the hand's bony mission;
his slogans scratched on postcards
with the angular angst and precision

of a graffiti artist about to be disturbed.
They fell around Berlin like dropped
ticket stubs – outside a doctor's surgery,
a lawyer's office – misspelt and sometimes
incoherent. *German people wake up!*

Two hundred postcards in two years.
Under the black wingspan of night
he hugged the dark like heroism, watched
from the shadows through lit windows –
we are all always almost on the other side.

He'd let a card fall onto an empty stair.
It lay like a missive to the whispering
loneliness from some deluded ghost, a call

to the stillness in one person's eyes as they
would scan the urgent ink like a ransom note.

Unseen, he stubbed out his cigarette on the wet
pavement, the sound like his father spitting
into hot coals. They were betrayed in the end,
Elise and Otto. Beheaded in Plötzensee Prison.
Everyone who found a card handed it in,

sent it away from them. Repelled
by the painstaking effort, the disjointed words.
Repelled by the passion, which is madness.
Which is belief in the power of writing.

KAZIMIERZ

In the Old Jewish Quarter of Krakow
it is November.
It is colder than –
almost too cold to breathe.

The roads trace a map of aftermath.
Where the street bends like a fractured arm
people still point out the house of a doctor
who treated everyone, regardless.

And the synagogue. The tombstone
of Rabbi Remuh, who could prophesy
the person you would marry,
duped into making promises he could not keep.

Suitcases obediently packed
with dreams of lavender fields,
thousands of families
believed they were going to France.

They stood in the square,
their thoughts turning like sunflower heads
towards the future tense.

Only their departure for Auschwitz
fifty miles away.
That alone is real.

Lately in Kazimierz
a glass roof collapsed under snow
killing seventeen people
and hundreds of tame pigeons.

Even this, so broken-winged,
does not bring us close.

GOOD BOY!
Independent, 8 January 2011

Maybe they *could* have
spied on the British
and reported to the Germans.

Since the nineteenth century
people had been 'teaching
dogs to reason'.

Don, the German pointer,
was famous for saying
Ich habe Hunger.
I am hungry.

There were experiments
in human-canine telepathy.

Kurwenal, the dachshund,
communicated in barking letter code.
On his birthday he was visited
by twenty-eight Nazi Animal
Protection Youth. He told them
he was going to vote
for *PAUL VON HINDENBURG.*

And Margarethe Schmidt
opened the Hundesprechschule Asra.
The Asra Talking School for Dogs.

Dogs were taught to talk and count.
Performances were held.
Hitler included them in his
Strength Through Joy programme.

A child said the dogs
could tell the time
and describe people
and correct spellings.

When a vet from the University of Munich visited
the animals could speak some words,
he reported, and could bark
or ring a bell for each letter.

One witness said it was like a circus.
Another that the dogs did not speak
because it was too cold.

Then there was Jackie, the dog in Austria
who mocked the Hitler salute
but got away with it
though files on him exist.

Their excitement at living,
their all-aquiver fur,
their scrutinising eyes
and damp discerning noses,
that fierce desire to please.

We should save our incredulity
for Heinrich Himmler
who, it is said, had his soft furnishings
upholstered with human skin.

GÖRING AND GÖRING
Daily Telegraph, 12 March 2013

It begins in Albert Göring's flat.
A small cramped flat in Berlin.
Albert Göring unaware
that the air is sodden
with the smell of depression.

It could be an ugly tale
about how the brother who cared,
the brother who would not hear
Heil Hitler uttered in his presence
ended his days soused in alcohol,
marrying his housekeeper
just before he died
so she'd get his pension.

Or a fable about the good Göring
and the bad Göring. Then
it could bring in
that time Albert Göring saw Jewish women
forced to scour the pavement on their knees
and joined them – on his knees
scrubbing; his self-degradation
alarming the Nazi soldiers
until they ordered them all to stop.

And the flamboyance, the generosity,
the hospitality, the dressing up
outrageously, a fur coat like a high-grade
prostitute wears to the opera, the intimate
knowledge of art, belief
in music, love of trees and living things,
all those protected species
and the hundred thousand acres of forest

and the arms smuggled
to the Leftists in Spain.

And a childhood echo:
the pain felt
when sent to boarding school,
a sensitive eleven-year-old
selling his violin
to buy a ticket home
from that imprisonment
and staying in bed
until they said
he never had to go back.

Except this wasn't Albert Göring.
This was Hermann Göring
who knew what was happening in the camps
and saw nothing wrong
with being on the winning side.

It wasn't the boys' fault
they grew up in Veldenstein Castle;
that their mother was von Epenstein's lover;
that Hermann Göring wasn't, but Albert Göring
might – or might not – have been
von Epenstein's Jewish son.

Anyway, it *was* Albert Göring
who got down to scrub the pavement
and helped the Czech resistance
and, after the war, had his list,
his little list of thirty-four
Jews he had saved.

Had saved by calling on his brother,
Albert Göring's big brother Hermann Göring
who let die thousands upon thousands

and who adored Albert Göring.
Never refused him.
Never minded all those times
when Albert Göring, to save a life,
signed himself *Hermann Göring,*

the camber of the letters
skewing the horizon
between the men,
letting the black-and-white
run into something unintelligible.
Something – if we could forget
we'd ever seen the dead body
of a Jewish baby
held up to the camera
like a badly made doll –
something we might have called love.

We heard about the Parisian brothels for the SS
burning up the curfew hours
with cigars and chandeliers,
the copulation chair, the Arab room,
the flower grotto, the Hindu chamber,
the champagne bath.
Exotic, erotic, narcotic nights.
Madame Jamet declaring *I am*
almost ashamed to say it, but
I've never had so much fun in my life.

That was not us.

And, later on, there were mouldering whispers
about the camp brothels:
homosexuals sent once a week as a cure;
each evening the women prisoners
forced to pleasure men every twenty minutes.
They were often sent to die, those women – even
if they survived the forced sterilisation;
the forced abortions.
Without anaesthetic.

That was not us.

We were the women of Limoges.
We worked in carriage 3544
of the Orient Express, acting out
its Art Deco fantasies in nine double compartments.

We were inspected for venereal disease
three times a week
by German doctors. We were
terrified of the rash, the discharge
that would have us branded saboteurs.

I wish I could say
they were young men, they
were human too, and tell of how
they missed home, were crying out for warmth,
needing their libido to push against death.
That he spelled out 'Liebling' with his finger
on my back.

Or that lust, cresting
before a military manoeuvre
hurtled us all into a dark frenzied tunnel
thundering towards an orgasmic light,
heartbeats driving the train's
phantasmagoric propulsion
away from the fire-twisted grimace
of metal and blood.

It was not only the war
which taught us to steel ourselves
before offensives –
the probings and penetrations;
stains drying on the sheet
like maps of conquered territory.

When the war ended
we were taken, shaven headed,
by our *own* people, marked with ash,
labelled 'horizontal collaborators',
sometimes numbered on our foreheads,
tarred, even.

The imprint of one man's buttons,
one army's insignia
is much like another
when it's pressed hard into your skin,
your soft shivering belly,
your stifled animate self.

HERMAN ROSENBLAT, AUTHOR OF THE HOAX HOLOCAUST
MEMOIR, *THE ANGEL AT THE FENCE*, JUSTIFIES HIMSELF
Independent, 16 October 2009

People liked my story.
Not everyone gets to be on Oprah.
It was a great publishing deal
what with my son in a wheelchair after the accident.

Primo Levi's book wasn't accepted for years.
And look what happened to him.

Clouds. Who is to say
what a cloud is showing us.
I was a child in Buchenwald.
I didn't understand to remember.

A dark raven was rare over Buchenwald.
Was that a vicious angel?
Come to taunt me with its sign?

I know the girl I was to marry
lived two hundred and ten miles away
and unaware. And didn't
throw me an apple each day
over the edge of reason.

But time is not linear.
Which of us can tell.
For this perhaps I was spared.
Many times since
she has saved and nourished me
throwing sustenance to my spirit.

Because none of us survived
without damage. We are all
living metaphors, fenced off from love.

Most people's existence is like bad fiction.
What was I to do?
Make an angel of the rotting corpse
of a prisoner left on the fence
where she threw herself

leaving a trace behind my eyes
like the smudge
a moth leaves in an unopened drawer?

The truth is so ugly.
And no beginning or end.

Was I to write a nasty nursery rhyme
from the eeny meeny mo
of standing in line
while a soldier's eyes
blinked some of us into phantoms?

Anyway – there is no language.
Not since that dread hand
pushed itself between the skin
and the flesh of each word.

I found a pea once in Buchenwald.
A wizened pea on the ground.
And I was elated.
But no one wants to read about that.
It was not even the colour of a pea.

And do you think an apple
– its skin whispering of orchards –
would have been anything but cruel.
Like that savage moment
when you wake from dream

to the bucket in the corner,
the water in the day's gruel
bursting your kidneys
and bloating your thoughts.

I did not die.
Perhaps I lived because I lied to myself.
Do you not see?
Perhaps the angel was the lie.
Perhaps the lie was the angel.
I was only trying to spread a little hope.

It was my imagination.
In my mind I believed it.
Even now, I believe it.

THE 2012 BEAUTY QUEEN OF HOLOCAUST SURVIVORS
Independent, 30 June 2012

Dreams – her number will come up.
Her favourite colour is smoky grey.
Knows what it's like to stand in line
waiting to be chosen.
Regrets – no regrets.
Believes – only in the future.
Thinks – the past should be closed off behind barbed wire.
Her song – the first bird she heard
on returning to Paris.
Perfume – *Eau de Cologne.*
Feels her sense of humour
and her God saw her through.
Her favourite food – lutkas
like her granny made
though she has to go easy
because of the carbs.
Would like to tell the audience:
I know what you are thinking.
But it's precisely because
   the cattle trucks,
   the no-end railway track
   the bodies and the sleepers and the bodies
   and the stench
   towards the end.

Precisely because I learnt
it is the distractions from the truth
that keep you alive.
That's precisely why I have the right
– you might think it vain and vacuous –
to be part of this spectacle.
Because that's what surviving means.

The Gingerbread House

Brigitte Höss, Daughter of Rudolf Höss, Auschwitz Commandant
Telegraph, 11 September 2013

We had a pond there, at Auschwitz.
And a picnic table.
My father took us to see horses
and German Shepherd dogs.

I was seven and he used to read me 'Hansel and Gretel'.
He was the nicest man in the world.
Sometimes he looked sad
when he came back from work.

We could see the prison blocks.
I remember men in uniforms,
black-and-white stripes,
working in the garden.

My mother loved that house
where we lived for four years.
We had cooks and nannies and chauffeurs.
She called it Paradise.

If somebody asks about my dad
I tell them that he died in the war.
It was a long time ago.
I didn't do what was done.

It stays with me.
There are crazy people out there.
They might burn my house down
or shoot somebody.

I sleep with my parents' photograph above my bed.
There must have been two sides to him.

The one that I knew
and then another.

I am eighty
and I have cancer.
I don't want anyone
to know my name.

Thomas Blatt

WHO TESTIFIED AGAINST JOHN DEMJANJUK AT HIS TRIAL IN 2010
Independent, 17 and 20 January 2010

Thomas Blatt never got used to the shock
of white scalp
as he shaved the women's heads,
his fingers mute witness
to the dreams beneath the skulls
of those, *he* knew, were about to die.

It was the words that kept returning,
sixty-seven years after his escape,
calling him to account.

The woman who didn't realise,
asking him not to leave her bald.

The woman who bent her head compliant
saying, *How can you do this?*

Thomas Blatt never got used
to the sounds of the dying
filling him like blown glass,
while his hands rummaged
through their clothes for gold,
along lapels and linings,
seams and hems.

Thomas Blatt was fifteen.
His father and ten-year-old brother,
his mother, were killed within hours
of arriving in Sobibor.

Haunting him still,
the last thing he said to his mother:

Und gestern durfte ich nicht
die Milch austrinken,
weil du etwas
für heute aufheben wolltest!

And yesterday I wasn't allowed
to drink the rest of the milk
because you
wanted to save some
for today!

THE HAND THAT FEEDS YOU
HANS LIPSCHIS, COOK IN AUSCHWITZ FROM 1941–1943, WAS CHARGED AT THE AGE OF 93 WITH BEING AN ACCESSORY TO MURDER

The steam in the kitchen
made the cooks purblind
as the hogs' heads boiled
for five hours to make 'Head Cheese'.

Hans let them cool
then scooped out the brain and cheek
from all the slippery concaves
and convexes of the skull.

He placed the meat
in dishtowels
and tied them with string.
These he soaked in a brine

of brown sugar and onion
and allspice and garlic salt.
And bay leaves and white pepper.
For two days, pressed down

with a board and a clean rock.
Then it could be sliced cold
and served with vinegar and pickle
and *graubrot* – rye bread.

The skulls he would boil again
for the prisoners' watery soup.
And he would add the potato peelings
from the soldiers' thick *kartoffelsuppe*

and the woody hearts of the cabbage
left over from the *brat* and *sauerkraut* casserole.
He utilised everything. And anyway
when the peelings were thrown away

some prisoner always retrieved them,
raw, and ate them rotting
from the rubbish.
When times were tough

he had to be inventive
with just tinned *fleisch* or *wurst.*
But at other times – roast mutton.
As the knife's serrations

scraped out marrow from the bone's 'o'
a sound like someone clearing his throat.
The kitchen had its own phonetics.
The diphthongs and gutturals

and double consonants of appetite.
Strudel. Pflaumenkuchen. Hasenpfeffer:
it was an art to demonstrate,
with surgical precision, how to dress,

disjoint and divide a rabbit. He
had an empathy with food,
as he leaned down to the ovens
to control the temperature

sensing exactly how much longer
the chickens needed for their skin
to blister crisply
over succulent breast meat.

He always kept the scraps of such meals
from the soldiers' plates
for the prisoners' daily soup.
Even sucked bones – saliva

would not matter to people who could steal
a morsel of bread from a corpse.

While he was on duty selecting
which vegetables could last another day

and slow-roasting old broiling fowl
– a goose, some shot ducks –
in foil with onion powder
to tenderise the tough bird

so that it would be palatable,
over one thousand Jews might arrive by train.
It was a fine large kitchen.
Twelve chimneys.

But it was not easy making food
to undernourish so many.
He could never be sure how many mouths.
A litre of gruel for each prisoner,

sometimes so watered down
that to get the slightest nutrition
so much had to be drunk
that it strained the kidneys.

And each prisoner had to get a portion
of *brot*. Every day.
Though when they could,
the kitchen staff held back

enough sugar and yeast
for an illicit fermentation
whose frothy kick brewed in them
the feeling they were in charge of their own patch.

It took the discipline of his visceral self
to manage, amidst all those bodies,
the culinary manoeuvres and strategies of food.
Otherwise the waste was unthinkable.

THE SAME RIVER TWICE
HERR SMOLEN, HOLOCAUST SURVIVOR AND FOUNDER
OF THE AUSCHWITZ MUSEUM
Independent, 4 February 2012

I was here before.
I returned to Auschwitz to live
with my wife
in the death camp
in the flat above the office.

When I was elsewhere
I grew weary of the mornings'
insistence on light.
I got lost
in my argument
against the anodyne
drift of summer roses.

Each day
the part of me
that is haunt
died away.
The truth was river-mist,
too beautiful
and disappearing.

Birdsong was a betrayal
of the orchestra
in my pulse
counting me into
oblivion and back.

I did not want to measure my remaining time
endlessly pacing out from memory
the lengths and breadths,
the scale of cruelty.

So I returned here.
To Auschwitz.
Where the walls demand no explanation.
Where I was let into the secret.
Where my warm breath can melt a patch
on the ice-patterns' blind crazing
between us and the past.

I can see the clouds
modifying themselves
and the sky.
But I do not need to remonstrate
with the earth – its unreasonable
fecundity.

Tattooed,
I can never now
be naked.

But here
I can make love
skin to skin
and nothing subtracts
from the numbers
I live in.

And then, as the roaring engine
of my blood subsides,
breathing quiets,
I am within earshot of the others.

I might fall into a helpless sleep,
sensing that we can all be still
in the knowledge it is over
for now.
In the dreadful knowledge
that we are real.

STATISTICS SPEAK FOR THEMSELVES
In 2006 one in every three Israelis over sixty was a Holocaust survivor.
Two in every three patients over sixty in Israeli Mental Hospitals were
Holocaust survivors.
Time Magazine, 14 January 2002

No matter that there is cerise bougainvillea
spilling over the door,
now it is too late
to forgive them our sins;
to forgive them
their grotesque knowledge.

Inside locked rooms,
trying to stay cool
lying on the bare tiled floor.
Or secured in solitary confinement.

Or sitting in foyers
grinding their jaws
juddering with shock and medication,
they rock.

We had no answer
for what their faces asked.
We had no room
for their shameful secrets.

Their bodies could house no more.
We reached for any anodyne word:
haloperidol, psychosis, thorazine,
depressives, schizophrenics. For sixty years

we shut survivors up
with the vicious susurrations
of savageries and sadnesses and silences.
Pitilessness.

Now, sometimes a cat or a dog
reminds them of childhood.
Sometimes stroking a cat or a dog
– Animal Therapy – lets them, slowly, regain
the power of speech.

Sometimes now, if the survivors
have relearned how to speak
– Testimony Therapy –
we let them say it.

For sixty years we blamed them
– the sordid unredressed
with their sundered senses –
for surviving so untidily.

Many of them
could have enjoyed rich lives.
They *could* have led a normal existence.
It is too late. It is too late.

WHAT ROGER GARAUDY CLAIMED
Independent, 25 June 2012

Disease killed millions.
Never extermination.
Holocaust? That lie!

'WE WILL NOT BE SILENT'

In a final delirium of defeat
a dying man in Auschwitz
incants hoarsely
with every outbreath
thousands of times
Jawohl. Jawohl. Jawohl.

In a basement flat in Munich,
students crank the hand-operated
spirit duplicator, its mechanical heartbeat
pulsing a wheezy subversion
into the fumes of solvent and purple aniline dye.

Thousands and thousands of leaflets:
If everyone waits until the other man makes a start …
300,000 Jews have been murdered in this country …
Each German is guilty, guilty, guilty – schuldig, schuldig, schuldig.

As close to weaponry as they came,
this metallic insistence on rightness;
a call to passive resistance
they thought as potent as the report of a rifle.

They risked all of themselves
and each other every time
they bought paper, or bought ink,
or bought stamps, or carried the leaflets

by train – clutching false identity papers,
or smeared tar and paint on gable walls:
DOWN WITH HITLER
a calligraphy of defiance
mired in night, which
took on dangerous substance
with the morning light.

They believed in the WORD –
Goethe, Aristotle, the Bible. Believed
their appeals would be caught on the updraft
of like-minded souls.

They could not accept
that language itself had been tamed.
All the syllables were already known to the police.

One moment's act of spontaneity
when Sophie Scholl flung a last handful
of frantic propaganda down into the atrium
of Munich University and was glimpsed
by the caretaker.

The members of The White Rose drifted as weightlessly
as petals to the floor of history.
The guillotine sliced through their idealism
as simply as through a ream of paper.

The night after they were beheaded
there was a protest by students
 – up to three thousand –
but it was a show of solidarity
with The Party.

As the adiline purple ink began to fade,
they dissolved into a collective dream;
perpetual tellers of a story to which
all the listeners were indifferent.

And then they were silent.

THE HITLERS IN ARGENTINA

Grey Wolf: The Escape of Adolf Hitler; Simon Dunstan and Gerrard Williams (Sterling, New York, 2011)

Adolf Hitler had very bad teeth.
And gum disease.
And halitosis.

We held up his lower jawbone,
his mandible with its dental work,
to mouth a mangled proof

that he did indeed
watch Eva Braun
bite into a cyanide capsule.

Shot his dogs.
Shot himself
in the bunker

in April 1945.
That the bodies
were burned.

Now, how can we bear them,
Adolf and Eva,
lunching by the lake

at Inalco, their mansion
in Patagonia, where they
might have lived until 1955?

Eating squab – baby pigeon –
and a favourite,
liver dumplings,

the Andes
whispering
Bavarian snows;

Adolf
winding a fork
in thick

wildflower honey
for the opening mouth
of his youngest daughter.

What did we expect
of God,
or of the Earth?

PRAYER IN DESPERATION

Dietrich Bonhoeffer
wrote his name
and his address
with blunt pencil
three times
on the pages
of a volume of Plutarch.

Dietrich Bonhoeffer
could not abide
the thought of taking life.
But in the concordance
of his conscience
he had found
that Hitler
ought
to be murdered.

Dietrich Bonhoeffer
wrote to his parents from prison.
The letter is full of disappointment:
not to receive any books today,
no matches, face cloths,
or towel this time ...
... some toothpaste please
and a few coffee beans ...
and from the library,
Pestalozzi, Natorp, Plutarch ...

Dietrich Bonhoeffer,
Lutheran Minister,
felt that to be holy
he must drink the earthly cup
to the lees.

'This world must not be written off prematurely'.
'It is only by living completely in this world
that one learns to believe'.
'We have to live in the world'.

So that,
at Flossenbürg concentration camp
on 9 April 1945,
he seems unready to leave.

Piano wire is sold by weight.
It is packaged in tight coils,
the steel made tensile by cold drawing.

He is entirely naked,
yet he kneels
for his last prayer.

It took, some say,
almost half an hour
before all the lonely questions
were fine-tuned to silence

'conversations that have never taken place'
'yearning for colours'
'yearning for the voices of birds'
'thirsting for words'
'the outline of a book I have planned'
'I cannot work unless I smoke pretty hard'
'I have been so often preserved in safety'

'no right to call anything our own'